IN A KINGDOM
OF BIRDS

ALSO BY
KEN FONTENOT

POETRY
After the Days of Miami
All My Animals and Stars

FICTION
For Mr. Raindrinker

IN A KINGDOM OF BIRDS

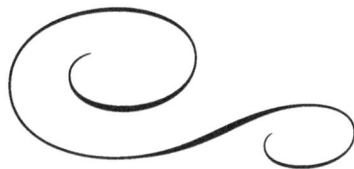

POEMS BY

KEN FONTENOT

PINYON PUBLISHING

Montrose, Colorado

Cover painting by John James Audubon

Book and Cover Design by Susan E. Elliott

Photograph of Ken Fontenot by Andrew Thomas

First Edition: March 2012

Pinyon Publishing
23847 V66 Trail, Montrose, CO 81403
www.pinyon-publishing.com

Library of Congress Control Number: 2012934040
ISBN: 978-1-936671-07-6

Acknowledgments

AILERON-ON-THE-WEB: "Shostakovich," "Bach, Mendelssohn, Vivaldi"

AMERICAN LITERARY REVIEW: "Looking Out My Small Window in Summer I See the Oak Prematurely Yellow"

AMERICAN POETRY REVIEW: "Mad March," "Any Father Speaks"

ANEMONE: "Internal Revenue Service"

BALCONES: "Our Lips Are Gates"

DI-VERSE-CITY: "Late Shift in the Morgue"

DI-VERSE-CITY-TOO: "Poets and Blackberries"

DI-VERSE-CITY-2008: "One for Rita"

ECOTROPIC WORKS: "Oh Wingbeats," "The Words for Containment," "Good Friday Near the Cow Pond"

GEORGIA REVIEW: "Remembering the Wind," "Dark Insects"

GREENFIELD REVIEW: "On My Mother's Side"

KANSAS QUARTERLY: "Wondering: All the Way Home"

KENYON REVIEW: "Return To a Spring Full of Little Boys"

LACTUCA: "A Study of Two Girls"

MAPLE LEAF RAG: "From a Son Who Knows Only Books," "How Dreams Arrive: On a Full Stomach"

MAPLE LEAF RAG III: "We Mention the Dead"

NEW LAUREL REVIEW: "Talk"

NEW LETTERS: "Trouble"

NEW ORLEANS REVIEW: "Each Day You Woke Still Pickled," "Late November," "My Nephews in May," "Reverie"

NORTH AMERICAN REVIEW: "Girl with Cat"

PERIPLUM/AUSTIN: "What Comes To Mind on a Day Cloudless as the Heart," "Considering Maria McGee"

PLAINSONG: "In the Presence of Sparrows"

SOUTHERN REVIEW: "A Fan Reminds Me of a Morning Long Ago"

TEXAS OBSERVER: "A Shrimp Boat in Port Aransas, Texas Calls an Aunt to Mind," "The World Without Me," "First Light"

VERSE: "Sweet Paper"

WELLSPRING: "Bees, Other Bees," "Consulting Rilke and My Grandfather"

WHAT HAVE YOU LOST? ed. Naomi Shihab Nye: "Drifter, Owl, Mouse"

"The World Without Me" also appeared as "Almost Asleep" in *Is This Forever Or What*, edited by Naomi Shihab Nye.

"Girl With Cat," "In the Presence of Sparrows," and "Shostakovich" also appeared in *The Glass Eye*, edited by Ken Hanson.

The last line of "In the Presence of Sparrows" was inspired by a line from an Elton Glaser poem.

My thanks go out to Barbara Hamby for her orchestration, her skills at gathering together this book in its present form.

Some of the poems in this collection have appeared in magazines under different titles.

To the Memory of My Father and Mother

CONTENTS

II. OUR LIPS ARE GATES

III. IN A KINGDOM OF BIRDS

IV. MAD MARCH

I. BLOOD NOTES

RETURN TO A SPRING
FULL OF LITTLE BOYS

Either I am (1) in the room, or
(2) out of the room with no
thoughts of rooms, or (3) out of
the room with thoughts of being
in the room. The mind produces
that wonderful third thing
for which we have no name.
In my later years, in my
years of gray hair
and pleated pants, I am going
to try to discover whatever
bond there is between thinking
and feeling. It will be
a limpid enterprise: pure,
sincere, and without beauty.
Preachers' children will come
to know other preachers' children.
Trees will come to know
other trees. We will accept
good soup for what it is:
good soup, not bad soup.
What did Brecht know about
poetry? A lot. What did
Rilke know about poetry?
A lot. The path is narrow,
but the path is long. The streets

are empty, but the streets are clean.
Does your mind jump from
one thought to another? Mine does.
What is poetry if not this leaping
through the water levels of the mind?
This sad, sad story of the heart?
Smarty Pants is what my mother
used to call me. My father
called me *Sad Sack*. I stayed
in the sack until I was
good and ready to get out.

That was Saturdays. Sundays
I hit home runs. Fridays
I didn't eat meat. Jesus
loved little children. I had
a BB gun that found its mark
in tin cans. A neighbor came over
one night. She held in her arms
a dead dog with a hole
in its head. She said, did you
do this, and I said, no, not me.

ON MY MOTHER'S SIDE

In Eunice, Butch stole cars,
held up stores, then did time.
At least two cousins
always wanted to borrow money.
And when they did,
never paid us back.
After which Mother said
I wouldn't lend money now
to my own Momma.

Once my Grandfather McGee
was so drunk, us taking
him home to New Orleans to visit,
that he cursed in front of us kids.
In Norco, Louisiana
my father stopped the car
to put him out.
We finally let him come in
out of the rain,
he beat on the door so hard.
He walked 13 miles.
At supper, wet and sunken, he said:
"I'll be a sonovabitch
if I eat your rice.
It don't have no goddamn gravy."
A lot of nerve, Pa Pa McGee,
who wrote my grandmother from jail,

his note to her in the blood
of the tooth he pulled
for the occasion:
"Mom, take me back."

A FAN REMINDS ME OF A MORNING LONG AGO

The fan watches over us,
its one eye moving back and forth,
back and forth all night.
And it's the night
that keeps us safe.
Even Faulkner, who stayed
up most nights, would have known
how conclusively good it is
to stagger to an easy bed.

My grandmother Beulah
used her oscillating fan so long
dust gathered everywhere about it.
It is the kind of fan you saw
in old magazines. It still sings.
It wakes us up with its whispering.

Somewhere out there beyond
the crawfish mounds, beyond the cows
bowing to their god, beyond the cow pond
and its menagerie, beyond the fields
that have let go, a squirrel awaits
his one lead bullet to freedom.
My grandfather and I in the shadows.
Squeeze, don't jerk, he says. I squeeze.
And the morning echoes.

CONSIDERING MARIA MCGEE

She was as faithful gardening as a surgeon
washing his hands. The North Star winked.
So did the moon, the dark clouds like eyelids.
Heaven gives in, she said, *the devil gives out.*
I know just what I want from this old world,
do you? Do you see the sky as just another
pretty face? Trees! Grass! They've figured out
how to make the animals happy. Which is every
concern of every whale that ever lived, their
sensibilities being less common than most. What
did the spoon say to the fork? What did the baby
bird say to the momma bird? She ironed.
She dusted. She watched TV. Hooray for every
puppy who ever lived. She read. She sewed.
She made love. What can you tell me
about the state of the earth? She raised
tomatoes. She raised horses. She raised children.
When will mothers ever be given their due?
          When doesn't the light around
their hearts ever warm our cold bodies?

MY NEPHEWS IN MAY

A few good things emerge from the TV's mouth.
The rest you can have. But my nephews
seem to have to watch. I want to tell them:
the TV is a bandit, but I settle for saying nothing.

My nephews love their dog. I love just sitting
as the Zen masters recommend. What's this?
I'd give anything to feel like a drunk, yet
without having had so much as one glass of wine.
Booze only simulates freedom. While time erases it.

In the old days girls winked and waved at you
from their cars. You could still walk
a long ways with your uncle, and it rained less.
But maybe this nostalgia has got it all wrong.
Maybe objectivity should be insisted on.

Today the May air is implicitly special and mild.
I expect the best from May as a teacher expects
the best from her student. For May is the most
diligent of months, since it has spring on her side.
Always making what we care about—bees, flowers, grass.
Always the right temperature, the one we'd like
to have year round. 60 degree nights, 70 degree days.

Again my nephews are playing soldiers in the yard.
For the time being they have forgotten about TV.
Childhood, after all, is meant to be excelled in.
By dreaming, by singing, by entering what vanishes.

MOTHER: THE FIRST TO RISE

The teeth have their own reasons
for rejoicing. So do the eyes. And me?
I say, let the rain come cause
the ground needs it. It's perfectly
fine the way you attend to
your difficulties. When it rains,
you cry. When it snows, you laugh.
But what would a fly, with its
tiny brain, know about *that*?
Our quandary is love, which believes
very little in the art of talking.
Like a newborn it can only feel.
So what? So read Kleist if you've
nothing better to do. He says
light has everything to do with pain,
and darkness has everything to do
with love. In my dreams I am six
again. Suddenly I am not in a dream
but half-awake, breathing hard in
the bed of my childhood. Mother gets up.
I hear her cough. I hear her making
coffee. I hear her opening things.
Eggs popping. The sun, too, is awake.
All morning it watches over our small house.
We'll lie in bed just a little longer ...

"ROBBING THE CRADLE"

You don't hear that expression much anymore.
Is it because older women and the young men
they marry have both become more free to choose?
My great-aunt was fifteen years older than Uncle Mike.
At forty she had a baby, which made him
a handsome twenty-five-year-old father.
Gossip everywhere. "Henrietta," they said,
"what the hell are you trying to do anyway?"
But she continued as if nothing had really happened.
Someone who could care less what others thought,
she outlived Uncle Mike by a good twenty years.
"Robbing the Cradle" they called it, with envy galore.
At quilting sessions the older women just shook
their heads. After all, ignorance falls through the cracks.

A SHRIMP BOAT IN PORT ARANSAS, TEXAS CALLS AN AUNT TO MIND

The boats return with their shrimp.
Dreams get wasted. Money goes fast.
Gasoline is high. Shrimp prices are low.
How can anyone make a living?

I come from Louisiana,
but now I feel like a Texan.
Think of all the people
who have to leave their homes
and go to other states for work!

The old man sits in his boat. Aransas.
A pipe. A son. Three dogs. Chickens.
He works his own nets. Fixes his own motor.
His wife knits. If *he* is not happy,
then she is. If he has lost his cat,
she has gained her son. *If the Lord wants me,*
he says, *I'll be right here.*

My aunt was a shrimper from Grande Isle,
Louisiana. I think I was ten.
In her small boat a gnat flew in my ear.
It hurt. I told her. She took a long draw
on her Camel and blew smoke in my ear.
Oh, Aunt Bessie, *that* got the gnat out.

FOR A YOUNG BOY WHO ASKS
ME WHY HE SHOULD STUDY

on a theme of Brecht

What will it take for us to see that spring
is really a messenger? That winter is aware
of much more than we give it credit for?
That nights are real because the stars are real?
It's nice to know the sky doesn't think less
of rain because the rain is sad. It's nice
to know that clouds are older than the heart.
Once I smoked, and someone called the cops
on me. I was a tiny boy. They told me it would
stunt my growth. The cops gave me a lecture.
What is peculiar to the heart is not
always peculiar to the mind. To see
a dove is not to see its bleak undoing—
there where the hunter finds its weaknesses …
What should I learn? you ask, your knowledge far
from over. I say learn everything you can.

DARK INSECTS

My house is dirty, but my pigs are clean.
My shoes are the color of soot, but my dogs
are the color of deer. Somewhere out West
the wind is filling a man's shirt. Nearby,
a woman on a horse is riding her fences.
I have touched the dead, but until that
first time I never believed they could be
as cold as stars. The dead: taciturn, sullen,
eternal. And why not? We give them nothing
worth talking about. The sky told us things
we always understood to be true: recall clouds.
We have considered the trees, wondering why
the birds abandon them for the air. We have
considered the oceans, wondering how they
keep the fish so happy. The world continues
only if men's thoughts complete their bodies.
My advice is don't give advice. It clutters
up the room like so many dark insects.
My mother could please any stranger. *Here
have some*, she said. Or: *If that's the way you
want it.* And my father? He did more things
than most men. It's nice to know you have
　　　　　uncommon parents.
It's nice to know that when everyone else
was asleep, your parents were busy thinking up
a world for you that no one else ever thought of.

CONSULTING RILKE AND MY GRANDFATHER

All that's in me, all that wants out,
also wants to have wings and feathers:
for which thought I thank no one,
though I have been reading Rilke.
He tells me: don't call attention to yourself.
He tells me: live your life without needing
a woman to serve as your mother.
He tells me: love your poems as you would
your children. All that's in me, all that
        wants out,
also wants to have stripes, a tail, and growl.
It's past knowing, this what-we-want-to-be.
What's pure desire, if not the wish to be
who we want, but on our own terms?
We work. We love. We dream. And the dream says:
wake up. It says: you're wasting your time.
It says: help yourself, for the world
leaves you little to fill your hunger. I can
remember my grandfather putting unwanted pups
to sleep with one, quick leveling of a hammer.
Painless. Bloodless. Behind the barn where
no one could see. But I saw. I ran away,
it troubled me so. Rilke would have said:
you should have stayed. You should have
watched. You should have let your eyes
meet your grandfather's eyes, and understood.

FROM A SON WHO KNOWS
ONLY BOOKS

Dusk doesn't settle in till the last man
is home from work. Working in America
means all the time you don't spend with
your family. It means supper's on the stove,
and you're nowhere to be found because
your boss is telling you he's in a rut.
Most all of us in ruts these days, the back
wheel spinning, mud flying everywhere,
the car stalled, going no place. It helps
to push, but what do you do when there are
                    not enough
around to push it out? My grandfather would
find sticks and leaves, or an old board,
and put it beneath the wheel
so that the wheel could bite. And luck? Hmm.
It's like dreams one has only now and then.
Those dreams a man can't really call his own.
My dad said: Trust the sky and what the sky keeps:
clouds. I say: Believe in trees. They're
                    solid, sure.
                    Long ago.
My father in the tops of trees: pruning with
a hand saw. Way up there I see how small
a man he is. How small a man he is
to be a father! What is it like to have
a son like me? I don't know. Will I ever know?

A man is happy with his gun, his boat.
A man is happy with his lawn, his dog.
Just think. I'll not grow up to be my father.

FIRST LIGHT

My mother smiles again in my dream.
What is she doing to me? Spanking me?
Suggesting I leave? Sheltering me
from the rain with her umbrella?
What? But I'm awake now and can't remember.
We spend our dreams like money:
sometimes they vanish forever.

Oh nothing will let us forget anyone like a mother.
Childhood friends reappear, too,
in the midnight movies of our unconscious.
Also there: fathers, brothers and sisters,
grandparents (if we knew them), uncles and aunts,
those not even the gods can take away.
Yes, if their lives didn't matter,
they would not be so much a part of us
as they seem to be, nightly, behind our eyes.
Could one even say a man who dreams
always of animals, wars, buildings, forests,
and rivers lacks an understanding of people?

Still, the trees seduce us. No doubt there.
Leaves too: the trees' wind chimes
which play their music only for the wind's sake.

Now the sky invents. The earth quickens.
Animals everywhere feel music in their blood.
Where has the darkness gone? It is morning.

GOOD FRIDAY NEAR THE COW POND

Look in each darkening window
of the line of trucks
groaning on the dirt road to Mamou
and you see a caravan of moons.
No rain since afternoon.
"The dust has gone to Heaven,"
Tante Néda says, her belly swollen months.
The catfish, headed and gutted,
grow hot, ripen in their pots.
Good Fridays mean *courtbouillon*
on everyone's plate.
In Evangeline Parish, in the South of it,
there are no terrible hills to climb,
but the heat *this* April is terrible,
and no one is speechless about it.
The heavy men, the small men,
talk and smoke and stir with big spoons,
their belts six or seven notches
on the good side of hunger.
The trees weep, the cows doze,
the dusk burns the woods
for a moment only.
The women know the sky's another face,
and their children swim nearby
in one dark window of the earth.

HIS EYES

Last night I appeared in my father's dream.
He told me so this morning, having wakened
all sweaty. I ask for details.
He says it was a bad dream,
and he'd rather not elaborate.
He says I'd better understand the world
somewhat from a woman's point of view
because the anima elicits mystery.
Lovely mystery.
His life has been like clouds passing,
one after another, sometimes white,
sometimes dark and stormy.

Last night I appeared in my father's dream.
This morning he cooked fried eggs for me.
Made toast. Buttered it. Poured me coffee.
Gray-haired, he stands calmly near the stove—
whistling, talking about love.
The light has started to take over the kitchen.
Such metaphysics. Cannot be agreed on.
So I have to admire him, a messenger
bearing at times good news, at times bad.

Last night I appeared in my father's dream.
Jesus how bright his eyes are.

II. OUR LIPS ARE GATES

ANY FATHER SPEAKS

Every fish—poor; but the trees do get better in spring.
We say: along these particular lines. Still, we mean:
along any lines that will allow us to get what we want.
After all, the harder a bow presses against its string,
the more tiring it becomes for the violinist. It's
uproarious, it's exhausting: the way the conductor
smoothes out the air with his hands (a flattering sort
of chap). Why did he get into this business, anyway,
since his parents wanted him to be in oil from the start?

Yes, we're always the last ones to know if something
exciting is taking place tonight. If someone were to
attempt to paint the moon black, we'd be in the dark.

Women in love teach more than love. They usually
offer the bird life of authenticity, hard to come by
these days. Then there are their children, taken up
and pressed into whatever they need, so long as their hearts
remain clay-soft and loneliness-blue. Have one
more child and the clocks start striking for you
at odd hours. Glinting, permanent. That's how the sun
calls nothing loss. For the sun never takes—it only
gives.
      We know how we *won't* live our lives.
How we *will*, how the bees make good honey—is another
story. But no story is as clear as a cat's eye. Not
even a father's story, delivered, raised, and forgotten.

LET'S GO OUT

When a poem begins, trees lose their leaves.
So, too, nighthawks begin their short songs.
It is always morning. It is never morning.
If we listen very carefully, we can hear it:
how one can mistake the squealing
sound a bus makes when it stops for
the high-pitched sound the universe
made when it began. All of which is now.
Listen again. You missed it the first time.
Your thoughts were elsewhere. We say,
enough of love, and we mean it. We say,
enough of money, and we mean it.
I wouldn't give one solitary cent for a new car.
You neither? Let's go out. The lightning bugs
are as bright as your eyes.
The night is as young as the world.

SWEET PAPER

The box of letters stored away years ago
in the attic—letters written to me I saved—
has become a lair for spiders, roaches, and lizards.
At the bottom of the box: roach droppings.
In the box: lizard eggs, hatched and unhatched.
Look, here's a baby lizard,
rummaging through the letters like me.
Surely these beasts thought
their home would remain forever undisturbed!
Oh secretive roaches, did the sweet paper
you bit into satisfy your hunger?
I think it must have.
Just as I think all those who wrote
to me years ago must now be living
either a different life or no life.
And these letters from a woman I once loved—
where is she now? Should I keep them?

LATE SHIFT IN THE MORGUE

What are the grackles saying,
they with their black throats?
I am here, in a room I have rented
for a month. I sweat. The fan
means more to me than a king's ransom.
The grackles can't keep from talking,
muttering vowels only a grackle would know.
I wonder where grief goes,
when it descends from us. I wonder which star
will accept my joy, when I bid it
leave me. Happiness works late shifts
in the morgue, you once said.
I don't agree. I think the cloud
which is our soul, drifts among bright
skies, is there, in one piece, rain or no rain.
You can keep from knowing the clouds
just as little as you can keep
from putting your pen to the page.
These are vague times, no time for wishes.
What, in God's name, would we wish for?

TALK

Talk to me about my vitalistic pessimism
or my eudaemonistic materialism.
The men to talk about me
would be Schopenhauer and Feuerbach.
What it boils down to is this:
a certain woman I like is avoiding me.
But if you want to talk,
we could talk about the Biedermeier
attitude toward life or even if you want,
about Austria's political problems in 1849.
There is a certain flatulence in talking,
the lips just baring the teeth, the eyes blinking.
There is a certain sadness in talking,
the throat holding absolutely everything it can.
My grandmother talked to please, my grandfather, to brag.
Sparrows talk to remind the trees of their impatience.
Squirrels chatter to let the grass know they're happy.
Once I left a pick-up in neutral, got out,
watched it roll down a hill, and smash into a tree.
I ran after it. No luck. My boss that summer said,
you numbskull, you could have killed someone.
He talked because he had it in for me all summer.
And once, outside a bar, I saw a man, in a rage
over some woman, put his fist through a windshield.
All night he talked to tell the stars he was alive.

OUR LIPS ARE GATES

Just what is enough? Not words. There can
always be more of those. Not promises: never
enough of those. We want softer songs,
gentler weather. Distance makes history
as affable as love. And without their Philosophy
of Worms, birds would be lost.

A thousand years.
Half a million years. What do years matter
to the dead? We give them back their old
blanket of snow, the one they liked as children.
Each of us has a prayer for the sky, a eulogy
for the forest. Our eyes are entrances. Our lips
are gates for the messengers of our words.

Grief: that child in cold weather without
a coat. It sings dirges. It writes elegies.
We with half our noses in shadow, half in light.
We with our bodies soaped and scrubbed.
The dark houses. Conversations in other rooms.
A fireplace. Of two doves
both will forage. Neither will wait.

A STUDY OF TWO GIRLS

At camp on Sand Mountain,
the summer I fed horses and did repairs,
I chanced upon two of the girls
in the woods, kissing at the foot
of a Loblolly pine, and I watched. The sun
peaked, its one wing of light almost blinding.
They did not see me. They were in
their sixteenth summers. How much,
I thought, this was like the parties
where the twelve-year-old girls
held each other around the waist
and waltzed or jitterbugged.
Wasn't this the same innocence?
My heart thrilled for those girls,
just as my heart thrilled
playing Seven Minutes in Heaven,
locked in a dark closet
with Becky Guidry, her mother
and all the twelve-year-olds
giggling just beyond the closet door,
their party favors whirring and whistling.
Later that summer the camp director
found out. He dismissed them from camp.
I was sad. I knew deep down
I could have loved both of them
although they could have never loved me.
Both of them wore red ribbons in their hair

and lots of funny rings on their fingers.
Having long, blonde hair,
they fit easily into tight jeans.
They rode horses every rodeo,
the saddles massaging their thighs.
How I could have loved them
although they could have never loved me!

Sometimes on my long walks home, even now,
I think I spot them walking across the street.
The dark center of their lives
has come full circle: they walk surely,
confident now in just the simple clothes they wear.

And to think I cannot even bleed when it counts.

TOGETHER OR NOT

We shall either never quite marry,
or marry again and again.

But the question remains:
does the bride have enough love
for two or more men?
Or the groom.
Does he have enough love
for two or more women?

And what about the other lovers:
man to man, woman to woman?

It's clear that most of them love blue skies
as much as each other.
It's clear that most of them praise the sun,
that miracle worker whose time won't
run out for as long as we can imagine.

Whatever winters lovers have spent together,
none has ever felt warm
except in another's arms,
the moon dropping behind the trees.

There are reasons for the heart to beat faster.
There are reasons for the mind
to go through a hard time.

We shall either never quite marry,
or marry again and again.

WONDERING: ALL THE WAY HOME

The physics of the water reminds me I, too,
am water. Less innocent, perhaps, less contrite.
But water. Goethe was right—this business, finally,
of everything going upward: water,
the direction of branches, a candle's flame.
In the end something called the Nightmare of Innocence
awakens us on cool November mornings,
awakens us just before the animals begin
with their delicate sounds,
with their uncommonly selective music,
with their huffings and their puffings.

And me, always, like the multitudes at first light,
grinning to myself in the mirror,
pulling my lips like this, furrowing
my brow like that, combing my hair with my fingers,
checking to see—beneath this blonde scalp of mine
that stands up often like Alfalfa's on *Our Gang*—
if I am the same man as I was yesterday.
In another life I would be a cowboy,
but now I am a man who looks at the stars
and sees in them angry eyes, *your* eyes,
in fact, you, who left me last night at some bar,
wondering *is he the same man I married*—all
        the way home.

LIFE AFTER DARK

I'm wondering exactly who is called
to a life after dark. Not me, for sure.
I'd rather be a Shostakovich listener in an easy chair.
And don't think I don't hear pain
in his string quartets, because evil is everywhere there.
Just as Young Goodman Brown
felt gloom even in his dying hour.

Oh the stars shine only for some of us.
While a few count their lives as time in prison.
My idea: people can certainly stay apart
like cream unwilling to mix with milk.
On the other hand, we have the bull
not able to see much past the cow.
So is that love, or just desire?
Or perhaps a combination of both?

But sometimes our fictions fall short.
The hero and his lover make us wish
we had stopped reading after a few pages.
For both demand too much attention from us,
so that we feel exhausted about mid-book.
Readers, after all, view the world most passionately—
as if their own lives were at stake.

HOW DREAMS ARRIVE:
ON A FULL STOMACH

Outside, in the dark, there is the hope of
a young tree to be part of the woods.
Which is like the hope of the kingfisher
to dream of rivers. The fog of desire.
The fog of sleep. It keeps watch all night.
What can we say of the past? That memory
was always a prisoner, released only now?
That life renewed itself everywhere but here?
In my house—I don't know about yours—
there is always the life that wants to grow
wings and leave the ground for the first time.
Our only wars: distant wars. A new thief
plans his evenings, alone and silent. A seed
lets go. A child holds a toy gun to his head.
We get full. We get full. And dreams
      arrive like shadows.

THE DISTANCE BETWEEN US

The rose smells fresher to a boy than
to a man. Youth welcomes youth.
Along the outer edges of creation,
along the inner folds of a flower,
and along the smooth skin of desire
men speak of this & that, of absolute
necessity. What is necessary? Birds, apt
to remember more than we imagine they can.
A cool creek. Clouds: meticulous and devout.
A just god which some of us call "nature."
There, where myth declares itself, where fathers
tell their children stories every day: there
beyond the treetops the sun makes everything
seem more fragile than daylight. You

      look at me. I look at you.
The distance between us is patience.

WE ARE HERE BECAUSE THE CLOUDS BELIEVE IN US

All spring I've been trying to get
to the other side of courage. Not this side
which has the dark shadow of a copperhead,
but the other side which is motley, pure,
and without emptiness. Always I see farther
than I can think, guess farther than I can know.
Evenings, especially these, when the moon has
more to share than the stars, I go out under
dark trees. To hear the crickets. I know
their music will outlive me. I know I will
have to be very patient to listen to their
entire symphony without taking a break.
And dreams? Dreams are like that: a place to go
for stories when the world has too few stories
of its own. Say we're here because the clouds
believe in us. Or because the stars knew us
in another life. I'm content to believe that.
Aren't you? I'm content to say I want to be
old, aren't you? In the silence of
a cool night the fields call to us:
come home, come home, don't they? Everywhere
and for most of the day we are busy putting
the heart aside for the mind. Is that what
you want? Not me. I want to be able

to feel my heart when I have to. And when,
as time allows, I don't want to feel my heart,
I want to give myself over completely to my mind.
I've been wading in the shallow waters
of courage for a long time. Now it is time to get
to the other side. Will you join me? Oh will you?

I PLAN TO GO TO GERMANY

A sky so blue the birds stand out.
What stands out too, a sun, a moon.
One and only one of each of them.
A gift is what I'd call this air.
So given it reminds us thus
of things beyond our need to sell.
If air belongs to everyone,
what price is there to talk about?
Any landscape reminds the self
of truth—what is or what is not.
I'm here, a town I'd never thought
to call my own. The strangeness of
the light, the profound strangeness of
the shadows means another night
has come and gone, my life a life
that wants only to age as well
as cheese. Today I'm fifty-seven.
I think of resolutions still
to make, of fathers whose sons have run
away from home. My country's sad,
I plan to go to Germany.
I know men, and I know their ways.
Marriages fall apart and still
they rise to cook their scrambled eggs.
Another wish, another journey.
So our lives remain largely our own.

III. IN A KINGDOM OF BIRDS

POETS AND BLACKBERRIES

Always the same story with us poets:
we're simply not treated well enough to suit us.
Think of the money owed to friends who see us
and conclude: "Here he comes again, wanting money."
You'd hope we'd have a little self-respect.
We don't. Hard to get along with, not even
our sisters can expect a pleasant word from us,
especially when we've had too much to drink.
The sun rises, and often we rise, too,
cursing the day for its false hopes.
But then we eat a fresh blackberry;
suddenly blackberries are gods.
In our poems we praise blackberries,
saying there was never anything their equal.
Our town becomes Blackberry Town.
Our world becomes Blackberry World.

The mail arrives. A bill we can't pay.
And it's as if blackberries didn't exist.

BACH, MENDELSSOHN, VIVALDI

It must be precisely when we have no thoughts
that we most resemble the animals, whose brains
must live in a skull of oblivion, an absence.
Yes, our *tabula rasa* might just equal our neocortex.
How hopeful I am that the brain's puzzle will soon
be solved! How hopeful I am that the body will heal!
And who knows the body's strength
any more than a resolute, brutally keen predator?
So I watch a pair of hawks land on a high power line
pedestal. Are they taking a break from their weary circling?
Soon they fly off. Oh to be able to emulate happily their lives.
An overcast morning. Almost no wind. A May Sunday.
The classical music station is my lovely distraction.
Some Mendelssohn. Some Vivaldi. Some Bach,
who was a family man as well as teacher-organist-choirmaster.
How did he find the time to get so much great work done?
The answer: he wrote music to fulfill a specific need.
But his biography doesn't explain why his work
makes me feel as if I were the father of a new child.

In my office it's the flickering of fluorescent lights
and the sadness of pencils that penetrate my thoughts.
And my window is only another kind of TV screen.
A child rides past on a bicycle too big for him.
A squirrel noses around in the grass for a nut.
Sparrows chase each other in the madness of spring,
not one of them God-fearing, or proud, or worried about money.

TROUBLE

1.

Anger wears a marvelous face.
The guy in the back seat
insults me for being late,
and I tell him, creep,
get the hell outa my cab.
I quit *this* job, *that* job.
Brecht knew about these shitty jobs.
He knew people in their worst faces;
he knew how anger wears a face
men can stand to see only in their dreams.
I think of Brecht bowing to his soup.
There's Trakl, too, like me
in his one and only suit.
And later, across an ocean,
there's poor Flannery O'Connor,
trying to explain her illness to peacocks.

2.

Who talks? Who listens?
Thinking is a kind of listening:
thoughts echo
from the darkness around the soul.
We think steady as our heartbeats.
The heart wants out!
Three million years now
and it wants to belong
to some other kind of body.

3.

The hottest day of the year.
And the first time
I've ever seen a sparrow panting.
In my pocket: 22 cents.
Not enough to buy a hamburger.
The dog sees the cat.
The cat arches.
It's the same story.
Some guy is getting mugged.
You don't want trouble.
You take another alley home.

INTERNAL REVENUE SERVICE

What can you say about a hundred desks
      in one room?
That they would look better if only Edward
      Hopper could have painted them
in his own shadow, his own light?
That they still dream of the trees
      which were their ancestors?
Me? Give me a soul. Any soul. I'm more interested
      in the girl in bleached hair,
thumbing the desk to the radio. I'm more
interested in the short man's bald head,
      how his wife chews him out every
morning for the sake of no one except maybe
the ghosts of the lawn, which are his
imaginary friends. I'm more interested in the heavy
      lady whose promises are as good as always
kept. I came here looking for a way out of
another life. I came here with nails
      in my pockets and no shine on my shoes.
They say great men started at desk jobs,
      and I, too, mean to make my beginnings
a sure thing, a thing of beauty and respect.
      This morning I walk in having had no sleep.
Eyes with black circles. A grumbling stomach.
A muscle that won't stop twitching. That's me.
      And my boss nursing his black coffee,
wondering what the heck he's gonna tell

his wife tonight to get his cheatin' heart
        off her mind. Don't ever believe
these sad stories commingle only beyond
        the TV screen. They are here among
the silent, among the speechless, among
the coffee-bound, just beyond
        the dark wastebaskets of America.
Oh Momma, I gots dem paper-pushin' blues!

WHAT COMES TO MIND ON A
DAY CLOUDLESS AS THE HEART

Unhappier men have seen unhappier skies.
Hölderlin's Hyperion wanted to die on the battlefield,
and we just drink coffee as if nothing had
happened. The sea is full of nouns.
The sky is full of verbs. But no syntax could
quite replace what the stars send down
in their wisdom. Why didn't we remain Catholics?
Why didn't we spend our money more wisely?
Divorce has statistics equal to crime's. If we were
bureaucrats we'd say "no government is good government,"
but for now government will do. We're long past
inner freedom, having known gurus and priests
of all kinds: reformers of the soul. Even therapists
are eking out a living in a world that hates
to turn its money loose. A wise man already
has his money ready when the waitress brings
the check. A fool has no thoughts of tomorrow.

OH WINGBEATS

There is so much that sometimes turns out to be
nothing more than music with the notes removed.
Even then I find the world innocuous, wonderful,
and without the slightest hint of displeasure.
Which is what Aristotle could have lectured us on.
Of course, I may be taking the narrow view of things.
Therefore, I summon only rapture from the clouds'
          disposition.
What else? I am getting older, but neither the months
nor the days can possibly make my life any more
workable, as I was saying, any more workable,
for September is already here, and I have done
little toward the dehysterification of my life.
Even if I noticed the moon, even if the sun
satisfied all my wishes, I would still be left
with just a few doubtful, inept meanderings,
which could mean that anything possible goes.

Look up. The weight of the light is everywhere
          we are not.
Oh wingbeats, you are doing what my heart is doing:
pumping hard for merely the sake of living at all.
The birds rescue my faith in them by taking the only
road they know, the air. And because they keep
falling, almost unnoticed, out of the gray sky,
we know another miracle has put birds in our
dreams, and has let us fly when we most want to.

THE WORDS FOR
CONTAINMENT

for Nancy Harris and Sunday afternoons

In my dream, moths are pursuing me
the same way they always have to touch us
in real life. Daylight brings the dream to an end.
It is not a question of which I would rather—
dreaming or waking. For both entertain me
unlike pure consciousness with its ability to tire.

So this morning I walk from one tree to another,
asking myself if this is what we were meant to do:
follow our thoughts out into nature
where the birds are singing for the sake of us all.
Since questions don't require answers, however,
        the mere asking is enough.

The landscape stiffens: bright forest, clear lake,
dew on the grass. This is spring. Everywhere
the biosphere is newly creating her little existences.
And why should I not be amazed?
Why shouldn't a certain plenitude overcome me?

Ah, the words for containment are few:
sun, moon, earth.

SHOSTAKOVICH

The bow is poised on the strings like a rifle.
First, dissonances. Then melody, and who
knows what else. Just this: someone is dying.
No, many are dying. The man inking in the notes
is not sure whether or not he can go on,
for tonight anyway. Get some sleep, he tells himself.
Politics: more real than any of his complex dreams.
He dreams a musician unable to stop from
sawing apart a violin, soon in pieces.
He awakens, bathed in sweat. Morning.
Not wine now, but coffee, pity, regrets. Look,
we are dancing, he thinks, his mother's face
surfacing in this reverie, in this cold country
where, from the pens of artists, only blood flows.

LATE NOVEMBER

Another day as a security guard.
In the Coke can I can hear bubbles
making their tiny dynamite noises.
I am reading the selected poems
of Tomas Tranströmer.
I pass my fingers over the print,
hoping some of his magic
will lift from the pages
and enter my fingers.
Imagine! A psychologist by profession!
But putting ink to paper
is what he likes best.
I have visited his Sweden only in my dreams.
There, too much ice for me, too little light.
I pass my fingers over the print,
hoping for a literary miracle.
What is there left for the words to do
if no one is reading them?
Will the "Yes" prevail? Or will the "No"?

THE WORLD, AN OLD MAN

The Asians have given badminton over to their spirits.
In Singapore a truck runs out of gas. In Kyoto
a woman gives birth to four boys. The chances?
Slim. Landscapes keep such cool eyes on
the trees. Skies press on. Thus art fell flat
in the Hundred Years' War. People then had time
for only faith, of which a farmer had as much
as a priest. And now? Some machine steals a man's
money and he curses. The world is an old man
just learning how to read. He is almost blind.
And the mind is having another of its dark nights.

IN A KINGDOM OF BIRDS

1.

New books. New glasses. Old reading habits.
Such is the way the world looks at us,
loosening its tie from around its neck.
Christmas is a place that is far away.
Easter is not a time either, but a place
where our mental gods take their vacations.
What should I expect from the morning?
Cold orange juice. Hot coffee. The same news:
read it. The world is no better off than before.

2.

Rapes. Accidents. Always an obituary page.
If I had my way I'd insist everyone
read a feature article about how a bird builds
its nest. Mother Robin would work
all morning gathering twigs. Father Robin
would gather the soft down and feathers
other birds leave behind. The nest
would represent a country, the birds: politicians.
Other birds, bigger birds, want the nest.
They come with a lot of squawking
and puffing of feathers. They come with
a lot of elegant, but pretentious twittering.
You can guess what happens, my friends.
In a kingdom of birds no one is safe.

REVERIE

So many feet make up the joys of centipedes.
My feet, on the other hand, have both
limited joys and even some pain
after I stand on them all day like a waiter.
And what is pain, anyway, if not misfortune
in excess, misfortune weighted down?
One confines oneself to the home,
or to the beach where walking on sand
is unique and inexpressibly pleasant.
The sun, in fact, would look better
wearing a hat to cover its bald head.
At sundown its red face could be a kind of blushing.
Can't kiss the sun, can't hold it
in our hands—as much as we'd like to.
So the day passes without misfortune, and in our minds
a reverie arrives, once and only once that way.

DRIFTER, OWL, MOUSE

It's a shame we have to train porpoises
to be like us. Rather, we should be like them.
And take the great gray owl. I would
like to follow it. To take its picture.
Elusive and stately. That's how I want
to be. No prisoner to the earth, but
a sky-captain. That, too, is what I want to be.
Did anyone ever believe the mouse could
escape the owl? Did anyone ever believe
only men could love? I would like
to take a caterpillar and turn it inside out
like a sock. To see what's there. To see
why it takes such innocence to spin a cocoon.
What is said is not always what is heard.
Somewhere a mouse prays in an owl's beak:
there a drifter puts a hole in the owl's head,
the mouse a death within a death.
This is the world none of them wanted.

BEES, OTHER BEES

When I get old, will my face frighten me?
I'll be a civil servant like my father.
Though I said at twenty-one: don't be like
your father. I miss my Mississippi River,
far away, the ships, the wharves and all.
I find myself in the middle of my life.
Pity quiet men. Misery could be playing
in their hearts. And what is scratching
but an effort to get deeper in the body,
to reveal the body for what it really is?
The coffee stains on my shirt amaze me.
My shoes, dirty around the soles, amaze me.
The light in the window is half-light.
The light on the grass is full-light.
The shadows assume their places like gods.
Don't give me a picture without shadow,
without that simple grief of the earth.
Long ago my eyes glistened, my feet
hummed to their shoes, my legs stretched
like swans' legs. Back then a rooster
was a prophet, and girls waived and winked
at you from their cars. Children took long walks
with their uncles. Bees respected other bees.
But now a song ends somewhere, somewhere
a pillow is being fluffed for the night.
Somewhere a young girl is beginning to know
      her own blood.

IV. MAD MARCH

MAD MARCH

Folks, there is so much to be separated:
wheat from chaff, love from sex, bodies from souls.
Thus even sinister angels are learning
to take the good with the bad.

Ah, on a clear night I have seen star after star.
My astonishment itself astonishes me.
For I am not content to munch on peanuts
when there is poetry around. Not content
to be a coyote in a world of hawks, sleek and deft.

On cue, the worms surface after a heavy rain.
I kind of admire the couple of atoms of oblivion
that should be circling in their tiny brains.
Sometimes I, too, would like to copulate with
myself. Yes, it must feel good, at home in the earth.

But that's no reason to renounce us whom
Nietzsche said had master and slave moralities.
For a man of his stature to lose his great mind,
I'd say his contemporaries just wished even more
it wouldn't happen to them: insanity humbles us.

Think, for example, how spring maddens the animals.
They have no choice—March is a feeling distributor.
It passes out love, excitement, ejaculations, kisses.
It is also known as the magnificent Dr. Feelgood.
I've seen many a March I couldn't quite comprehend.
Then again I prefer sassy March to dreary December.
Just look at how a strong wind can change
anybody's mind. People want to wear the wind!
So stick around, March. We need you as the zoo
needs to have a lion escape every once in a while.

LOOKING OUT MY SMALL WINDOW IN SUMMER I SEE THE OAK PREMATURELY YELLOW

Bitterness on the tongue means bitterness
in the heart. Your grief is swollen
like an abscessed tooth. How simple
it would have been for man if his God
had sought him out as a friend. But no.
The father never seeks out the son
first. It must be the other way around.
And who, among either many or none,
prays for the father? Outside it is summer.
Anticipating fall, the oak has a patch
of yellow leaves. So. This is what He
has left us. Trees to admire. Animals
to eat. A window to the world, small and dim.

EACH DAY YOU WOKE STILL PICKLED

Addressing the air at dawn, I found everything else
silent except the radio I had meant to turn down.
Another parched summer, another cloudless day.
You: no longer among the living, a ghost.
"I need a funny story from you," I said.
"Tell your memory to speak," you said, invisible.

I never did learn what became of your body.
You had little money. Did they turn you into ashes?

Yours was a blessing only vodka would bestow.
Without it you could hardly breathe,
as if someone kept pushing you underwater.
You understood what Thoreau wrote about simplicity,
but not what Goethe wrote about moderation.

Still, I should have insisted. I should have said:
Bill, I won't stay here and watch you die.

ONE FOR RITA

I'm not going to set this poem in any particular
milieu. Rather it could be anywhere or possibly
everywhere. It is a time when mothers tend
to their children, foxes heave great sighs on the run,
and passion envelops the distance spring brings along.

You are ten or perhaps twenty. Your legs ache. You
possess fleeting memories of carnivals gone too soon.
It is either February or December, neither having
mattered much. A car waits in your driveway day
and night. Several giants have been calling a name
you barely recognize as your own. Nor is modesty
one of your virtues. The President is speaking.
He is talking about responsibility, which you believe
you have much of. He apologizes perfunctorily. The world,
he says, belongs to ... You know the rest already.

Once you rode horses. They died, however, in your dreams.
Once the sky was blue, but now there is no name you
can think of to fit what color the sky is. Suddenly
you begin to walk backwards. A child trips and falls.
No matter how hard you try, you can't catch her in mid-air.
And what is the significance of grace? You believe it
accounts for everything that can't be explained in
terms of just *love*. The world is bleak. The world is
glorious. You go on pursuing drowning men in every
city. You go on filling your jar of hope with yet more hope.

THE HOUSE OF THE BODY
for Julie Kane

Especially now, especially when the earth
builds its small fire in the West,
it's important not to blame the trees
or the grass for what we are not, or
even for everything we lack, because
      the land
asks only that we grow with it, that we
understand a bird is not bound to one tree,
just as the soul is not bound to one room
in the house of the body. Flowers darken,
shadows lengthen, bees dance to survive,
and there are one or two men who have
dreamt an explanation of the universe,
but they can never remember those dreams.
Other men, on the other hand, are
      content just
to build their own houses, and take
a short smoke once in a while. Me?
      I'm content just
to touch the wrists of slender girls, girls
      with
freckles and flaming red hair. Also I like
to watch sunsets like this,
              knowing such heat
could warm me,
            knowing I could even live
in such a city as that soft light makes.

REMEMBERING THE WIND

The wider the sea, the happier the whale.
Few whales are bad enough, but think of
the whales that get beached! See the birds?
They are companions to the night. They know
how grief is bluer than the sky.
It seems the intellectual dwarves have
taken over. And who would want it
otherwise? We are content with those
who claim simplicity is better than
knowledge. Give us the gentle embrace of
the wind and we will be happy.
Give us the cool nights of November,
and we'll trust the earth once more.
Which is not so unusual considering how
November, like a dream, welcomes everyone.
We move out of our houses. We leave
and arrive again. In a strong wind we are quick
to remember all the other winds of our lives.

WE MENTION THE DEAD

The people are asking for something different.
A black sun. A moon that never resembles
an executioner's axe. The kids still dream
about being old. The grown-ups still dream
about being young. When winter came the trees
closed down their shops. They had better things
to do than just look pretty. All of which explains
a lot, but not why doves must always forage.
Rain for three straight days. We speak of
onions and presidents, of flowers and bombs.
How self-assured the clouds seem: bitter
and sullen and full of grace! We speak of
passion and new shoes, of lemons and naked bodies.
Oh, how long will it take for the deer to feel
truly at home, to feel as if the clouds mattered at all?
We have made new promises, only to break old ones.
We have mentioned the dead, as if they were alive.

A DARK BEDROOM

I'd like to have a sky all to myself.
Or a whale, persistent and finicky. A whole
world waits for us at the bottom of the sea,
a whole dark bedroom. The sea: memory.
And longing too. Mother to passion, it welcomes
the night home, as if from a long journey.
Often I have ridden over waves, wondering
what it was like to sail the very bottom.
Who lets herself go anymore? Who doesn't?
Who believes the earth is greater than
what the earth dreams? The earth is not
greater than what the earth dreams.
For it dreams rocks and grass, which we
can't do without. We have considered
mountains and how they are ends. We have
considered boats and how they are means.
The day is old. The moon is wise. The sea is harsh.

A DREAM WELCOMES EVERYONE

I have imagined deer coming out of the woods
to meet only me. Deer the color of bark.
In a dream patience comforts its opposite.
Desire enters. So does ambivalence. Both
have lead roles in our play: a country play.
The stage: earth. A dream welcomes everyone.
Which is not to say why the dead refuse
to sing. Which is not to say why we send
the sky our regards. I love voices that
believe in wholeness. The voices of whales.
The voices of clowns. I love faces that don't
try to keep secrets. A fox face. A horse face.
If this is the outer world, what should
we say intuitively about the inner world?
Desire is one thing, passion another. I have
imagined deer coming out of the woods
       to meet only me.
See how they envy their shadows.
See how even the ground is theirs.

WE ARE WATER

The sky's miscellany: blue, white, purple, orange.
The tree's miscellany: green, brown, red, yellow.
Of course all depends on whether it is fall or spring,
winter or summer. Remember, too, that colors—
all colors—would not be there without the light
whose essence is still not powerful enough
to take away shadow—that decent foil to light.
Oh it's easy to see how our own anger erases
our best perceptions, those which let us
grasp the fundamental meaning of the world
and its brief successes.
                                    Still, no one knows
better than the whales what the sea
contributes to our total understanding,
for the whales sense implicitly those generous
things water offers us as a gift: why, we *are* water!
Except for the few proteins which contain it.

In order to comprehend why the days fill us
with so much desire, think of birds mating
in the air. So brief an encounter it is,
so unlike humans who would compare
love-making to the playing of a violin.
No, if the birds have given us an art,
it is not copulation, but songs bursting
forth from them as if from a summer storm.
Even one song a day would suffice.
But imagine! Songs everywhere.
Especially in the concert halls of the trees.

IN THE PRESENCE OF SPARROWS

Nothing grows in the fields of my hand.
Its fields are barren and damp.
Years ago the soul memorized its one poem
and told it to the hand, giving it hope
in a time of little hope.

When did the first eyes see?
Had the trees yet kept
their first promises to spring?
The way of the world is this:
the sea has its own ideas.
It does not ask for ideas
from the sky or the trees.
And in its one long ripening
the earth does what it does best:
consoles the few for the loss of the many.

Beyond the open window the sparrows quicken,
only their songs discouraging the snow.

A KNOCKING AT SOME DOOR

to Yannis Ritsos, with admiration

To gaze into a stone is to gaze
into a swimming pool of silence.
A tree thinks about blooming.
We think about power and having fun.
A tree thinks about food, about
how generous the sun has been and how
generous a leaf can count on the sun to be.
We think about babies, death, the rent.
We are not even in a class with the tree!

Your old men weep. No one answers a knocking
at some door. This one was smiling. This one
was shouting. This one was smashing
her dishes against the wall. This one was
turning a spent cartridge over and over
between his fingers. Oh, Ritsos, how dark
your country got when I was here
burning effigies of Nixon and drinking
good, cold wine and eating expensive steaks.
Ah, surely I am not like the winter trees.
The winter trees? They stand in prayer.

THE WORLD WITHOUT ME

I am close to my bed. I am close to my book.
I am close to my chair. And my silence lights the room.
There is no other real joy but this:
to feel as if a glass of milk were warming
inside one's stomach,
to pick out familiar tunes of Tchaikovsky
and hum along,
to wish the best for the world without me.
For I'm elsewhere, about to enter sleep.
All the lullabies I ever heard beckon me.
All the fairy tales and nursery rhymes
my mother—she was forever at my bedside—
filled me with return like a messenger.
And I say to the children of America:
Take comfort. Someday, you, too,
will treasure your moments of sleep—
even more than your parents promised.
Someday the pony who visits you
will be your companion again.

GIRL WITH CAT

In the window across the street
there is a face everyone would recognize:
a young girl holding her cat, looking out.
The sun almost gone. Her face darkens.
Perhaps she has already touched her own blood.
It would be nearly that time.

She recalls a prayer she said
to herself as a ten-year-old.
May my life be given a chance
to know a safety only God knows.
Serious, but intuitive.
More undaunted, more unpredictable
than any prayer of someone this young.

And the cat: captive, willingly so.
A beast too poor to own
more than one suit of clothes.
Fire-red, it licks her fingers,
so that she is a bit startled
at its sandpaper tongue.

What dreams of her her parents have,
assuming she will live
the better part of a century.
What patience the sun has, planning yet
another appointment for tomorrow.

www.ingramcontent.com/pod-product-compliance
Lightning Source LLC
Chambersburg PA
CBHW030711110426
R18122000001B/R181220PG42736CBX00004B/5